GW00372428

Also by Rob Parsons, OBE

Let Me Tell You a Story

Loving Against the Odds

Bringing Home the Prodigals

Teenagers! What Every Parent Has to Know

The Heart of Communication

The Heart of Success

The Sixty Minute Family

The Sixty Minute Father

The Sixty Minute Grandparent

The Sixty Minute Marriage

The Wisdom House

What Every Kid Wished Their Parents Knew

...and vice versa

Rob Parsons & Lloyd Parsons

With
Harry, Lily, Evie, Jackson & Freddie

Published by Care for the Family, Tovey House, Cleppa Park, Newport,
South Wales, NP10 8BA.

cff.org.uk

First published in Great Britain by Hodder & Stoughton in 1999.

This edition 2024.

ISBN 978-0-9955596-8-4

Typeset and designed by Max Randall www.maxrandall.com.
Printed and bound by Xpedient Print.

A Christian initiative to strengthen family life, offering support to everyone.
Care for the Family is a registered charity (England and Wales: 1066905;
Scotland: SC038497). A company limited by guarantee no. 3482910. Registered
in England and Wales. Registered office: Tovey House, Cleppa Park, Newport,
NP10 8BA.

Acknowledgements

With thanks to Dianne, Becky, Paul, Kate, and the brilliant team at Care for the Family. Special thanks to Harry, Lily, Evie, Jackson and Freddie - your additions are fantastic!

By the time I realised my father was right, my children were telling me I was wrong.

– Henry Winkler, The Fonz

Introduction to the updated edition

It's hard to believe that Lloyd and I wrote this book together twenty-two years ago. It's even harder to believe that Lloyd has now been married for eleven years and has three children of his own!

I remember when he was in his mid-teens and driving me crazy. One day, in desperation, I decided to reread every book I'd ever written on parenting and none of it helped a jot. (Which I quite understand is not a great incentive for you to go out and buy the books!) And it was at that moment that I did a deal with God. I quite realise that one is not meant to do that but, as I said, I was desperate. I said, 'If I can see him with a child that stamps their foot, shakes their head, and says 'No' – you can take me then.' Lloyd's kids are brilliant, but I think it's fair to say that he has seen the occasional stamp of the foot, shake of the head, and once in a while a negative response to whatever he had asked to be done. I don't want to sound smug or insensitive, but it's hard to describe the sheer joy of seeing one's grandchildren occasionally behaving exactly as their parents used to, and seeing a look of bewilderment on your child's face as if they are saying, 'Where did they get that from?' To say that I sometimes incite my grandchildren to misdeeds would be to take it too far, but suffice to say that we are very close, and what often binds us together is the knowledge that we have a common enemy.

So here's the original book, which we've kept mostly intact along with the cultural references of the time, with the addition of some report cards written by the grandkids that score their parents. I must say that Lloyd's look remarkably like the ones he used to bring home from school!

– Rob Parsons, 2021

When Dad told me that Care for the Family were going to re-release our book, I thought I'd better have a quick look to remind myself what I wrote all those years ago. I can't believe I said, 'All these books on how the parents are supposed to bring us up as angelic children who do everything right ... I don't think they realise that this is never going to happen, so I came up with the idea that a book should be written saying that our parents aren't as perfect as they think.' What was I thinking?! I've been lucky so far in that my kids have read about as many of my books as I used to read of my father's! If they ever find a copy, I'm sunk.

But of course now they will, because someone in Care for the Family had the bright idea of the kids writing report cards for their parents. I know that my sister's two children have done some of these as well. Katie always was the goody two shoes, so I expect she'll pass the parenting exam with flying colours. As for me, I've told my kids that if they write the truth I'll ground them for a month and stop their pocket money. I'm pretty sure Evie overheard me saying that to somebody and whispered to Lily and Freddie, 'Let's still do it. It'll be worth it!'

– Lloyd Parsons, 2021

A short word from Lloyd - 1999

When my father told me he was going to publish another book on parenting I thought there must be something wrong with us kids.

All these books on how the parents are supposed to bring us up as angelic children who do everything right and who are always hard at work for our exams. I don't think they realise that this is never going to happen, so I came up with the idea that a book should be written saying that our parents aren't as perfect as they think. This book is designed to help them realise the pain they put us through with their long lectures and boring speeches.

At first, the book was designed solely for kids to **strike back** at their parents but my father told me that parents needed some defence. So occasionally the old man will butt in with his piece to defend all parents. When this happens, all you have to do is skip those pages and go on to the decent stuff.

At last I think we've got them worried.

A long word from the old man - 1999

 Lloyd, I remember the day that you were born so very clearly. There were lots of things that were on my mind at that time like decorating your room, buying enough baby milk to sort out half the infant population on the planet, and getting an announcement in the local paper to tell everybody who already knew and cared, that you had been born.

But if I'd had any sense, it wouldn't have been those things that concerned me. I should have been worried about how I was going to be a father to you. As you know I was a lawyer; this involved me in acting in murder trials, company takeovers, and lecturing all across the world. Son, I can tell you, with not a hint of exaggeration, that nothing has come close to the challenge of parenting you. Don't get me wrong: you haven't been a difficult child – you didn't have to be. You just had to be a child.

As you know, I've written books on parenting, done countless interviews on the joys of fatherhood, and generally sought to encourage other mothers and fathers not to give up completely. I confess that sometimes I've felt like Arnold Schwarzenegger speaking about ballet. You may find this hard to believe, but there were moments when I felt I had really blown it as your father. At those times I have not wanted to give seminars on parenting, I have craved to attend them.

But, you know, Lloyd, all that has been good for me because in reality there is no such thing as the perfect parent. All of us – the 'experts' and the 'authors', the 'agony aunts' and 'ordinary parents' – are trying desperately to work out how on earth we are going to bring up this person for whom we are responsible and who reminds us every day that when it comes to parenting, we are in the beginners' class. And you know the really frustrating thing about being your father? Just about the time I learned how to handle you as a toddler, you stopped being one. And just when I had the twelve-year-old sussed out, you decided to be a teenager. And now – just now, when I am a world authority on the hormones of puberty – you are almost eighteen and you're grown up.

Do you remember how the idea for this book started? You said to me one day, 'You know, Dad, it's just struck me that parents spend the first ten years of a kid's life trying to get him into bed and the next ten trying to get him out.' We laughed and then one of us had the idea to share the great wisdom that you and I have learned over these past eighteen years. When we had covered the back of a postage stamp with that, we decided to ask some other kids and parents to help out. Thank goodness they did.

The thing **teenagers** say most about their parents

 They never listen to me!

The thing **parents** say most about their teenagers

 They never listen to me!

Dad, I know I can come to you with questions on the meaning of the universe and stuff like that, but can I ask an easy one?

Why is it such a big deal that my room is tidy?

Son, that one is really easy to answer.

1. I know it's your room, but it is in the same house as us and plague spreads.

2. I think something is moving under your bed.

3. We've had complaints from the cockroaches.

4. Some of that food under your computer seems to have turned to penicillin and it's important we get it to the people who need it.

5. I still think the Labrador we lost is in there somewhere.

6. I think something has ***stopped*** moving under your bed.

7. Some of the underwear in the corner may have come back into fashion.

Stupid things that **parents** say

Don't come running to me if you
break your leg.

Where did you lose it?

Eating fish will give you brains.

Don't be childish.

Son, can you help me with something that's been troubling me for
years ... I'm sure it's no big deal but it's eating away at me and it's best
we sort it out. It's just that on the very day you hit eleven, another person
emerged in our relationship. I call him 'Everybody Else's Father'.

I first came across him when you wanted to sleep over at Billy's house. I had
never heard of Billy and frankly there was precious little information coming
from you. For all I knew, a sleepover at Billy's could have been in the same
category as a night on the town in Soho. I said, 'No.' And it was then that
the character who was, in future, to make regular appearances in our lives,
stepped out of the shadows. You burst into tears and said, "'Everybody Else's
Father'" is letting them go.

You slept over at Billy's.

Since that fateful day this mystery man has poked his nose into just about every conflict you and I have ever had. 'Everybody Else's Father' lets his child go to a disco the evening before the GCSE maths exam. 'Everybody Else's Father' lets his offspring get ear, nose and belly-button piercings. And 'Everybody Else's Father' gives his kids amounts of pocket money that make me look like I need a visit from Marley's ghost.

The strange thing is that, although I thought I had met the parents of all of your friends, I have still not come across this man in the flesh. In fact, so far as I can tell, all the other parents are just about as scared, stingy and boring as me.

So here's the deal for the future. Next time you resort to using this character, I'll agree to whatever you want so long as you produce him. I mean real, live 'Everybody Else's Father' in my living room. And even if that means I have to agree to your doing that bungee jump off the Eiffel Tower, it'll be worth it.

And when you're gone, and there's just me and 'Everybody Else's Father', I'm going to ring every parent I've ever met and tell them I've caught the guy, he's locked in my garage, and dying to meet us all ...

When I was five, they gave us silver stars in school. When I was six, they gave us gold ones. When I was seven, I discovered you could buy stars in stationery shops.

— Jamie, aged 10

Things you wish your **teenager** would say

Is the music too loud?

I'll pay for my own phone calls
(look, I've written them in a notebook)!

I'd like to share some of my feelings with you.

If my friends phone, tell them I'll ring them
back when I've finished my homework.

You sit down, I'll do the washing up.

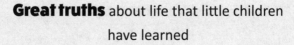

Great truths about life that little children have learned

No matter how hard you try, you can't baptise cats.

When your mum is mad at your dad, don't let her brush your hair.

If your sister hits you, don't hit her back. They always catch the second person.

Never ask your three-year-old brother to hold a tomato.

You can't trust dogs to watch your food.

REPORT CARD

COMPLETED BY:

Jackson

AGE:

<u>7</u> YEARS

SUBJECT	COMMENTS
BEDTIMES	Mum and Dad are very generous with bed times and let us stay up quite late, especially on weekends and me and my brother have learned some tricks to extend our bedtimes.
FUN	My mum and dad are extremely fun. They put lots of effort into it and definitely don't need to improve.
SAYING NICE THINGS	My mum and dad say nice things lots of the time. Except when my dad is angry - for example, when he loses a favourite game he really shows it. My mum is great too but when we do something naughty she shouts.
FAIRNESS	My parents are sometimes fair and sometimes unfair, like when they make me go to bed early that's really unfair.
GRUMPINESS	My parents are quite grumpy sometimes, like when me and my brother stomp and run around the house Dad gets really grumpy. Normally they're OK though.

Lloyd, every parent has seared into their brain some memory that, when recalled, causes them to begin to sweat, shake and generally want to hide. I have seven of them. They are your parent-teacher evenings. Even now, as I mention them, they come rushing back at me in Technicolour detail. I see a large school hall and parents in lines waiting to speak to teachers who sit behind large signs: 'Mr Wyatt – Maths,' 'Mrs Jones – Geography,' 'Madame Corvette – French.' As I get nearer the front I am able to listen in to the conversations that parents are having with the teacher. Phrases drift back down the queue: 'A delight to have in the class,' 'A triumph in the school play,' 'Have you considered Oxford?' And then suddenly I am face to face with Madame Corvette or one of her colleagues. They begin with, 'Ah, yes – Lloyd! Well, Lloyd is lively in class.'

I mumble, 'Thank you.'

'It wasn't a compliment,' Madame Corvette replies.

I remember begging a geography teacher to keep his voice down.

I stand and take the tirade and when it is finished make my way back through the line of parents mumbling, 'Great personality – I'd far prefer that to academic brilliance.' I confess, at times I would have settled for your having the personality of Attila the Hun for the sake of a couple of A stars.

But then, when I am at my lowest – buffeted by German, history and double-award science – there is always the sports teacher. An oasis of encouragement in a desert of despondency. I say, 'Speak up, I'm a little deaf.'

When I returned home your mum would say, 'How was it?'

'Not bad,' I'd reply, 'so long as we're happy to settle for a genius at rugby with a great personality.'

Dad, I wouldn't have done this to you if you hadn't gone on the attack, but Mum helped me find that box full of your old school reports. Can I simply say what a privilege it is to have such an academic as a father.

GENERAL REPORT :— Final % -45.44 .
These results clearly demonstrate that his promotion has not been justified. He is making no use of what little ability he has. A disgraceful report.

not good enough!

Signed, W. P. Lewis P. A.
Form Master

A. SINCLAIR, M.A., M.Ed.
Head Master

Date 8th April 1963.

Signature of Parent or Guardian :—
M Parsons

Date 11th April 1963

'Making no use of what little ability he has' – poor show, Dad. Old W. P. Lewis certainly knew how to build a boy's self-esteem!

Dad, I remember the first drag of a cigarette as if it were yesterday.
I was petrified. The first thing I did was to spray my hand with half a bottle of Lynx and then swallow three packets of extra strong Polos. I had always been so against smoking and then within a matter of days the pressure had got to me. It was the pressure I had resisted for so long. I just didn't have the bottle to stand up to my mates.

After the first drag I then went on to smoke one cigarette, then two, then three a day. I always used to look up to the people who smoked as if they were my role models.

Thinking of it now, it strikes me that this was the worst decision I have ever taken, and to make things worse I even had to lie to you to save my own skin. There were times when I had to say, 'Well, everyone on the bus smokes, that's why I smell.' I think this was the worst part of it. The lying used to scare me more than the smoking. I used to think if you found out I smoked I would let the family down, but if you thought I was lying you would never trust me again.

I remember the time when I almost got caught. I was walking down the street when you pulled up, tooted your horn, and I literally had to crush the fag in my hand. I can still feel the burning in my hand as well as in my stomach. Do you know, the ironic thing now is that I used to look up to people who smoked and now I am looking up to those who don't.

Lloyd, I well remember the row we had that night over your smoking.
And you're right, it wasn't just the cigarettes – although that worried me
enough – it was the lying I really found hard to deal with.

The **best** thing ...

I think the best thing parents can do with their kids
is be real. Not try to make out that they know it all,
all the time. Own up when they really haven't got
a clue. Admit their weaknesses and the things they
find hard. Even the things they're afraid of. Not tell
their kids to do what they don't do themselves and
most importantly admit it when they're wrong. By
the time you're a teenager you've discovered your
parents aren't the perfect people you thought they
were when you were eight anyway. So why should
they feel they have to keep up the pretence!

- Baz, aged 16

Lloyd, here are some questions I've being dying to ask you:

1. When you were small, why were you always sick next to the toilet?

2. Did I see one of your friends on *Crimewatch*?

3. Do your grunts mean anything? Is it a language? Can I learn it?

4. What really happened to Happy the hamster?

5. Did I see you on *Crimewatch*?

Dad, I'll tell you what really drives me crazy; it's when you and Mum jump to the wrong conclusions and accuse me of something I've had nothing to do with.

I remember when I was twelve I was building a fire with one of my mates and I snapped the branch off a tree and cut my arm. I came home bleeding and smelling of smoke. You interrogated me as though I'd been involved in a brawl while smoking a packet of cigarettes. You don't do it so much now, but sometimes it made me feel guilty when I hadn't done a thing. Worse than that, I think it destroys trust.

Things you wish your **parents** would say

 Would you like to borrow the car? I just filled it up.

Why don't you get your nose pierced at the same time?

We're out Saturday night – why don't you have a party?

I trust you.

Dad, I know that as long as there are parents and children there will always be lectures. The thing that parents don't realise is that they are so boring because they always go on about the same things.

Son, you have no idea how boring.

Screaming on the inside

My mother never really listened to me, never really encouraged me to talk about how I felt. It was as if she always wanted everything dealt with quickly and efficiently. She always seemed too busy to really take time to understand. I would be screaming on the inside. It was like being behind plate glass, not being able to make her hear. I'm sure it's why I find it hard to talk now. With some people who I know are being real and are really listening, I can. But I still find it easier to write my feelings down. The paper has time for me. It waits and listens and doesn't dismiss what I have to say. When I have kids I hope I remember to wait for them to say what they feel.

- Zoe, aged 17

More things you wish your **teenager** would say

"

Don't worry about getting me those shoes, Mum - I know they're far too expensive!

Do we have to have a television?

Are you sure the museum is shut on Saturdays?

"

Dad, the question that really used to annoy me was, 'What did you do in school today?' I know it seems daft, but very often I just couldn't remember. And then you used to say, 'Well you must have done something.' Well, I know I must have done something, but nothing that seemed worth remembering at a quarter to four. I could have told you about the fight in the playground, or the fact that Charlie got caught smoking behind the toilets, but if I had we'd have had half an hour on whether I was fighting or having a drag with Charlie. So I always used to say, 'Just stuff.' I'll bet if you went to most people as they left their offices and factories and asked them, 'What did you do today?' they would say, 'Just stuff.'

Girl in cafe:

'Hey Johnny, what you rebellin' against?'

Johnny (Marlon Brando):

'Whaddaya got?'

- From *The Wild Ones*

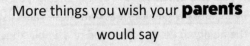

More things you wish your **parents**
would say

If we remove that desk from your bedroom,
we could get a wide-screen high definition
telly in with surround sound.

You're one of a kind.

Ten pounds is not enough; come on,
take twenty.

Why don't you start a band?

Lloyd, can I tell you the hardest part of parenting you? When you were a toddler I was sure I would look back on those years as the worst by far. You had the ability to get the attention of a whole supermarket if you didn't get your way at that very moment. I remember being with you at Malaga airport in the days before it had things like air-conditioning and seats. The plane was five hours late and you just rolled around on the floor of the departures hall, alternately whining and pulling your sister's hair. But I was wrong about those years being the worst. Since then there have been times when Malaga airport, on a hot August day, has looked like a vision of heaven.

When you hit thirteen I was sure this was it. It was as if you'd read somewhere about how teenagers are meant to behave and decided to do it all at once. On the eve of your birthday I said goodnight to a smiling, talkative, twelve-year-old. How was I to know that during the night, gremlins from the teenage farm were going to work you over? When you woke for school the next day you grunted at me. What I didn't know then was that this grunt was the high point of our communication – from there it went downhill.

But even that didn't come near the hardest part. It's not easy to explain, but let me try. When you were smaller I had real control over you. I was bigger for a start, and if I shouted you would sometimes look impressed. And I had lots of goodies in my armoury with which to keep you in line – the threat of going to bed early, or being grounded, or, for major transgressions, a visit to your auntie. But as you moved through your teenage years it dawned on me that so much had changed. When you were sixteen I could still send you to bed early, and ground you, but, in one sense, only with your cooperation! And if you really had ever decided to stay out until twelve when I wanted you in at eleven, there wasn't a lot I could do about it. Do you remember that one brush we had where you almost squared up to me? There we were like a couple of stags daring each other to make the first move. I still kid myself I'd have won, but I don't think I'd put money on it.

No. Whatever rules there are now will stand or fall not because I'm stronger, or can shout louder, or threaten you that Father Christmas only visits obedient children, but on the relationship that you and I have.

Don't you agree?

If you don't agree, go straight to your room (if that's OK with you)!

Kids tell it like it is on the big issues ...

Washing

My mum's always trying to get me to have a shower and wash my hair. And I hate doing it. I think it should be up to me. The thing is, I don't really want to be dirty or smell or anything. I just wish she'd let me choose when I have a shower and not keep sniffing me and saying, 'When did you last have a shower?' I feel like something that's gone off. She makes me have one always on Friday nights which is daft because I go to football training on Saturday morning and get all muddy again! Then she makes me have another one!

Give us a break

I wonder sometimes if my parents realise the real mix-up of emotions that we feel. Sometimes I love them so much and just want to go and give them a big hug. The next day I can't believe they could be so stupid, or mean, or back in the Dark Ages.

Why can't they understand that while it's true that 'I'll never learn', sometimes they don't either! It's as if we're straddling this bit of our lives like a fence. One leg wants to still be a kid and get their OK, running back for reassurance now and again. The other leg can't wait to be off clubbing or getting on the ferry to France without telling them! I just want to say, 'Give us a break and we'll try to give you one.'

- Emma, aged 15

Lessons every **parent** needs to know

 If you hook a dog leash over a ceiling fan, the motor is not strong enough to rotate a 3-stone boy wearing underwear and a Superman cape ...

... it is strong enough, however, to spread paint on all four rooms of a twenty-by-twenty foot room.

Playdough and microwaves should never be used in the same sentence.

Superglue is forever.

REPORT CARD

COMPLETED BY:

Evie

AGE:

_8_ YEARS

SUBJECT	COMMENTS
POCKET MONEY	We have learned that if we want pocket money we need to ask Mum as Dad is too tight.
GRUMPINESS	Mum and Dad sometimes wake up in the mornings and are very grumpy.
FUN	Mum and Dad are very fun.
GENEROSITY	Mum and Dad are very generous.
MOBILE PHONE	Mum and Dad could improve on their phone. Mum goes on Facebook all the time and Dad plays snooker and golf. Dad is improving with regard to his mobile phone use although he is still often on it even when he is sat on the toilet — that is very true.
OVERALL BEHAVIOUR	Mum and Dad are both amazing cooks and cook delicious meals for me. They don't need to work on the cooking skills.
SOME POSSIBLE IMPROVEMENTS	Bedtimes

The first half of our lives are ruined by our parents, and the second half by our children.

– Clarence Darrow

Lloyd, when you were fourteen you begged for a dog. When I think of the sweet naivety with which I said, 'Well, Lloyd, if you have him he's your responsibility. You'll have to feed him, walk him and take him to the vet's.' You assured me that you would be so dedicated to these tasks you would hardly have time for your friends or to listen to music.

I thought you might like to know that he's still alive.

But it's not all negative. Robert Benchley said, 'A boy can learn a lot from a dog: obedience, loyalty, and the importance of turning around three times before lying down.' Here are a few others:

- Never pass up the opportunity to go for a joyride.

- When loved ones come home, always run to greet them.

- When it's in your best interest, practice obedience.

- Let others know when they've invaded your territory.

- Run, romp and play daily.

- Be loyal.

- Never pretend to be something you're not.

- If what you want lies buried, dig until you find it.

- When someone is having a bad day, sit close by and nuzzle them gently.

- Thrive on attention.

- Avoid biting when a simple growl will do.

- When you're happy, dance around and wag your entire body.

- No matter how often you're scolded, don't buy into the guilt thing and pout ... run right back and make friends.

- Delight in the simple joy of a long walk.

Drugs

My dad said, 'You've never seen any drugs, have you?' I knew that he just wanted me to say 'No, Dad!' because then he'd feel safe and as if he had nothing to worry about. He likes everything to be cosy and manageable. Truth is, loads of kids in my school take them and I could get him anything he wants so I told him so. He yelled at me then as if I was already facing death as an addict. I'm not, I've got too much sense. He didn't see that just knowing where to get it doesn't mean you are. He couldn't see that he should be glad that I've kept on the right side of it all and learnt how to deal with the pressure. He just gave me a whole load of don'ts and a rambling lecture. To be honest, most of what he said was so out of date and so incorrect it wouldn't have helped a bit anyway.

- Dave, aged 16

!?

You can tell a child is growing up when he stops asking you where he came from and starts refusing to tell you where he is going.

– Anon

They take away the **fear**

The thing that most parents forget is that drugs do work. They do give you a buzz and for a short time they take away the fear, insecurity, loneliness and pain that so many young people are feeling. It's no good saying to kids, 'Drugs are a bad thing, they don't work anyway,' because kids will see instances where they do. Soft drugs do make people feel happy, more obliging, more at peace with the world and themselves. 'Just say "No!"' isn't enough. It's not working. Kids are too smart to take that on board. They need to be given accurate information and the benefit of the wisdom of those who have been there, done that and know, really know, what it's all about; people who will still give them the truth about how drugs can screw up their lives.

Adults have to stop being self-righteous about it and admit that loads of damage is done to their bodies by misuse of alcohol or tobacco. But kids, who generally have a strong awareness of injustice, are pointing the finger at supposedly older, wiser adults and accusing them of double standards.

All of us have to address what we are doing about the feelings of loneliness, low self-esteem, 'unlovedness' and pain that young people are experiencing and which might be turning them to drugs in the first place.

- Kate, a youth worker

Dad, why does Mum make such a big deal when I leave dirty dishes in front of the television or my trainers, and sports kit in the middle of the living-room floor?

Lloyd, because she's just tidied it and when you leave your mess behind you say, 'The job you do doesn't matter.' Sometimes she even interprets that as, 'And you don't matter either.'

Even more things you wish your
teenager would say

Mum, you sounded brilliant singing in the bath – you should go on *The X-Factor*.

No, midnight is too late, I'll be back around ten-thirty.

You want to go to a film, Mum? My treat.

I filled up the car for you.

Lloyd, some more questions I've been dying to ask:

1. Why are you late for school, church, and the dentist, but never late for your casual job?

2. Why did you stamp and kick for a year to be allowed to have your ear pierced and then let the hole close over a fortnight after you finally did it?

3. Do those trainers actually come off at night?

4. If you're embarrassed to be seen out with me, why aren't you embarrassed to ask me for money?

Dad, bullying is one of the worst things that can ever happen to a child in school. Luckily I was in a small school so bullying was not a big problem and it was not something that I had to worry about. For some children it is. Often it is the kids that think they are hard and have to prove themselves to others that end up being the bullies. I remember when I was accused of bullying and although it wasn't true, I still felt ashamed. This is because I knew bullying was going on and I still did nothing about it.

Now, I look back at the kids who were being bullied and I realise how brave they were and how brave they had to be. They had to come into school every day knowing that they were going to be bullied, but they still came back. Now to me that is the sign of a really brave person. But this might have been stopped if a couple of us had showed the bully who was the coward. There is only one person it can be: the person who has to humiliate someone else to make himself look big.

Nobody understands

When I wake up in the morning the first thing I feel is scared in my stomach. The same girl has bullied me for six weeks. People say 'tell the teachers' but they don't understand that you've got to have a life outside of school as well. I don't know what the answer is. Nobody understands how I feel.

- Meg, aged 13

Kids tell it like it is on the big issues ...

Food

If I can't stand the taste of tuna, why does my mum keep telling me it's lovely? She serves tuna flan up and says, 'Do you want some?' I always say no. She knows I'll say no. And I know that she knows that I'll say no. But she still does it! It always goes like this:

'Tuna flan?'
'No thanks, Mum.'
Serves everyone else.
'Sure you won't change your mind?'
No.
'You won't grow.'
Well, I'm as tall as her already ... and still growing.
'You have to eat.'
I do ... just not tuna flan.
'It's lovely, you know.'
Well, I don't think so.
'You don't know what you're missing.'
I do.
'Mmmm, it's so tasty, you should have some.'
I shouldn't. I'd be sick.

Even at the end of the meal she says, 'You know, you really missed out not having that tuna flan.' And I just want to scream, 'I don't want tuna flan. Not now, not next time, not ever as long as I live. I hate tuna flan!!!'

"

Children are natural mimics who act like their parents despite every effort to teach them good manners. They seldom misquote you. In fact, they usually repeat word for word what you shouldn't have said.

– Anon

Lloyd, do you remember the night I listened in to one of your phone conversations? You were about thirteen and talking to a friend I suppose I didn't really approve of. I hid behind the door in the room next to the phone. When I heard you were about to finish, I rushed out of the room and into the living-room and plonked myself down in front of the telly as if I'd never moved.

I have to say it – you were cool. You came in, sat on the chair opposite and watched the programme for about three minutes. And then you turned to me and said, 'You were listening in to my telephone call, weren't you?' Suddenly I knew how you must have felt when you were seven and I caught you painting the rabbit.

I remember word for word what I said, 'I am so sorry – I will never do that to you again.' You were pretty good about it but it did get me thinking. I once met a father who told me he had never, and would never, apologise to his children over anything.

It reminded me of what must be the silliest saying ever to come out of Hollywood; it was a line from the film *Love Story* (way before your time and fifty times better than *Titanic*)! 'Love means never having to say you're sorry.' The truth is that when it comes to rebuilding relationships, 'sorry' is often a pretty good place to start.

Even more stupid things
parents say

" Sticks and stones may break my bones but words will never hurt me.

School days are the best days of your life.

Winning's not important, just enjoy the game.

You'll soon get over it (when you're thirteen and the most gorgeous girl in the class has just dumped you).

Don't do as I do, do as I tell you.

A zit on your nose is not the end of the world.

Look inside

Mum and Dad are always on about my friends: who's a good friend and who isn't, who I should and shouldn't be seen with. They want to know minute details, not just of my life but my friends too. Who lives where, who does what. One boy they think is really rude, another one's 'a bad influence' and a third just smells as far as they're concerned. But these are my friends and I like them. When I was little they were always saying, 'You can't judge a book by its cover.'

- Heather, aged 14

The wisdom of **kids**

I believe you should live each day as if it is your last, which is why I don't have any clean laundry because, come on, who wants to wash clothes on the last day of their life?

- Tom, aged 15

Give me the strength to change the things I can, the grace to accept the things I cannot, and a great big bag of money.

- Harry, aged 13

Home is where the house is.

- Chloe, aged 6

When I go to heaven, I want to see my grandpa again. But he better have lost the nose hair and the old-man smell.

- James, aged 7

Kids tell it like it is on the big issues ...

Kissing aunties

I have to kiss horrible powdery aunties. Mum and Dad say I never have to do that but when I go to our big family Christmas party I have to. They say, 'Oh, you have grown since last year' as if that was unusual and, 'Have you got a kiss for Auntie?' Why don't I ever pluck up the courage and say, 'No, sorry, I've run out'? Sometimes they are just powdery and flaky. Sometimes they smell awful too. One auntie always holds my hands really tight and she has bony fingers that grip you. I like the aunties, I just wish I didn't have to kiss them. The uncles are much better. They don't get you to kiss them. They just pat you on the back so that you nearly fall over. Falling over is a better bet.

More great truths about life that **little kids** have learned

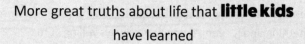

Reading what people write on desks can teach you a lot.

Don't sneeze when someone is cutting your hair.

Puppies still have bad breath even after eating a Tic-Tac.

Never hold a duster and a cat at the same time.

School lunches stick to the wall.

You can't hide a piece of broccoli in a glass of milk.

Dad, I used to think when I was small that you and Mum loved Kate more than me. It was always me that got the blame when we were caught doing something and it seemed you were always yelling at me.

Lloyd, probably the greatest challenge of parenting that Mum and I have faced is coping with two children who are so very different. Kate was what the parenting gurus call 'compliant'. That meant, Lloyd, that whereas you would lie on the floor of the supermarket and yell until you got your way, she would help to load the trolley.

While teachers would avoid me at your parent-teacher evenings, at Kate's they just wanted to touch me.

And, yes, I can understand that it was easy at times for you to feel that we were constantly down on you and not your sister. The truth is that when there was trouble you were normally at the centre of it. But let me tell you a couple of things that Mum and I vowed, early on, that may have just saved the day.

1. We would never say to you, 'Why can't you be more like your sister?'

2. We would look for the special gifts you had and praise you for them. They turned out to be many.

3. When at thirteen you hit your worst anti-communication, grunting, 'don't-ruin-my-life-by-acknowledging-me' stage, we still kept trying to get through.

4. We told you every day that you were loved.

A **lone** parent

Helen, you have no idea how tough it is sometimes bringing up you and your brother on my own. I know that we love each other but sometimes I feel I've blown it. I'm not sure whether I'm going through the same as every parent or it's because I'm on my own. It's harder all round. The money's always tight and I'm trying to be your friend, your mother and your father. I'm not complaining. I think I just want you to know how hard I'm trying.

- Helen's mum, Penny

Kids tell it like it is on the big issues ...

Being told what to say

❝ I love my mum but she doesn't seem to realise that I know how to speak and I know what to say. When we meet people in the street she says, 'Say "Hello," Pete.' I know that's how it goes. 'Hello' was one of the first words I learnt to say.

If someone gives me something, before I can open my mouth she says, 'Say "Thank you," Pete' and makes it look like I forgot.

When I go to a birthday party she says, 'Don't forget to say "Happy Birthday".' It makes me feel like saying "Merry Christmas" just to ring the changes.

So ...

Hello, Mum. Can I just tell you, you needn't worry. You've done a brilliant job with me. You're a great mum. I do remember what to say. Thank you ... and Merry Christmas. ❞

REPORT CARD

COMPLETED BY:

Freddie

AGE:

_7_ YEARS

SUBJECT	COMMENTS
POCKET MONEY	Mum and Dad need to improve on the amount of pocket money we earn.
GRUMPINESS	Dad is grumpy. Mum not so much.
FUN	Dad and Mum are both very fun and do not need to improve.
HELP WITH HOMEWORK	Mum and Dad are very helpful but not at a teacher's level.
GENEROSITY	Not so Dad but Mum is much more better.
USE OF MOBILE PHONE	24-7 a week.

There are three stages to a man: he believes in Santa Claus; he doesn't believe in Santa Claus; he is Santa Claus.

— Bob Phillips

Interfering again?

You slammed the door on us as you went out tonight. We'd just asked you where you were going and you said we were interfering, but really we think you know the reason why we asked. We care.

You know we worry about those two girls you're friends with. We're never sure where you are when you're with them. We don't like how you behave when you get home. Can you try to see that it isn't that we don't want you to have friends. It's not even that we don't want you to have those two particular friends. It's just that we want you to make the best of yourself and do what makes you feel good about yourself. We're not sure they help you do that. Why don't you bring them back one night, if that isn't too embarrassing? It might give us a chance to try to get to know them. We want to feel happy that you're with them. And that might start with you being happy to bring them and us together.

- Jenny's dad, David

Be patient, Lloyd – just a couple more questions that have really bugged me:

1. Why does one bank manager have to write so many letters to one teenager?

2. Why do you always shout 'Yes!' when a cash dispenser pays out?

3. Why do you lose every book token you are ever given and file every iTunes gift voucher in a file marked, 'Music – Purchases Pending'?

4. How come I'm such an expert on other people's kids and you still surprise me, worry me, and make me laugh almost every day of my life?

Dear Mum and Dad

I know it must be hard to talk to your kids
about sex but I needed you to try.
I learnt my lessons from my mates.
It wasn't the best place.

- Sarah

From a mother

Suddenly I know you're not a little girl any more but a young woman because ...

I can't tell your pants from mine in the ironing pile without peering at the labels.

Finding a tiny spot on your chin is a national emergency.

Who the paperboy was matters more than what he was delivering.

We giggle at 'girl things' together and it's us two women against the world!

You make me a cup of tea and ask me if I want a biscuit.

You close your bedroom door behind you.

You are only young once, but you can stay immature indefinitely.

– Anon

The day we **cried** in school

We found out about Will in school. We'd been asked to miss assembly to talk to our form teacher and the Head. They asked us, 'I wonder when you last saw Will?'

Well, we had to think a bit. He usually met us by the newsagent's in the mornings, but if he'd slept in or his dad hadn't left him any money for the bus he wasn't always there, so we got used to that. We knew he'd turn up later with his hands stuffed deep in his pockets, grinning under his fringe as he wandered in late. Most of the teachers had a soft spot for him so he always got away with it.

He'd been to the DVD shop with us the night before, but he'd wandered off before we'd chosen something. We thought he'd seen Clare walk by or something. He'd fancied her for ages and just didn't seem to get it right when he went to ask her out. He had this habit of just saying what he felt, and while some girls understood, she didn't.

Our form teacher was nervous, pulling his nose and looking intently at us. And we thought, 'What's he done? What's going on?'

He fell over his words as he told us Will was dead. We knew then that Will wasn't going to amble in, making excuses for his dad. That he wouldn't ask what day it was because he genuinely didn't know. Something in you wants to laugh, because for some reason it has to be funny if it is something to do with Will. Then there's this sick feeling in the pit of your stomach when you realise it isn't funny at all. All the sounds outside in the corridor disappear into the distance and your ears start drumming.

You wonder why the day hasn't stopped and why Miss Ferris is leading teams across the playground for hockey.

Doesn't she know? Will is dead.

You listen as you're told that he took aspirin and cider down to the boating lake and just sat there and did it. You feel so angry because you wonder why nobody decided to go boating last night instead of watching a DVD – as if you would at ten thirty at night. Daft things come into your head like whether he took his bike and whether someone would have nicked it by now. Then you wonder exactly where he is anyway. Now. At this moment. Because he should be sitting here with us, hearing about this guy who couldn't bear the fact that no one would listen to what he was trying to say. And got fed up with trying to say it. 'Come on, mate,' you wanted to shout, 'tell us now.'

But you know he can't do that. It's too late.

Then some girls are crying and if we're honest we are too. Clare goes home with her friend and the rest of our day is cancelled. We're given the chance of talking to someone if we want to and we wonder if Will was given that chance, and if it would have made any difference. Later, we wonder if Will ever had anything that he really asked for. Like his Dad worrying if he had his bus money, or friends who would accept him exactly as he was. Gentle and forgiving and tolerant and just too good for the rest of us.

Nobody wants to take the short cut by the boating lake home and a video doesn't seem like a good idea.

We want to ask Will what he'd like to do tonight.

- James, aged 16

Dad, of all the bits we had in from kids I think the next one is my favourite.

Remote control

One of the things that would be most useful for me in life would be a remote control marked 'life'. I could carry it around all day in my pocket. Then I could fast-forward all the difficult times and go back to the good. There would be more time for everything so I would be able to work my best and never run out of time and energy. I could freeze-frame parties and shopping trips and make them last ages and fast forward and skip my parents being a pain. If something funny happened with one of my teachers I could freeze it and we could all have a good laugh for ages. But the best thing would be to be able to re-run all the best bits again and record over the things you'd like to have another go at and not get wrong!

- Lois, almost 12; original idea, Benjamin, 9

Dad, this is what one of my mates said about his parents:

I am really proud of my parents. I wish I could find some way to tell them. They both work really hard. My dad is a social worker and I know he has a really tough time with some of the people he is trying to help. He doesn't get a lot of thanks for it but somehow he never gives up hope. It would be so easy to. My mum helps children with additional needs and you can see they love her a lot. The two of them really want to make a difference in other people's lives. They never say, 'You don't know how lucky you are' or 'If you saw what I saw every day.' They accept us and love us and even though the house is always a tip we seem to scrape along together because Mum says it's people that matter and she's right.

Are you jealous?

Yes, son, just a bit ...

Do I look all right, **Dad?**

There you stood in Doc Martens, purple tights with holes in, an old skirt of Gran's and a school pullover your mum had shrunk in the wash. Your earrings didn't match and you had what looked like a length of electric cable wound round your left wrist. Your hair – that beautiful auburn hair – was now only auburn if I squinted hard, although most of it still seemed to reach your shoulders. Your eyes looked as if you'd done a round with Tyson and your lips as if you'd eaten a bag of red jelly babies in record time. Yet you were beaming at me in expectancy, longing for my approval. What would I say when you said, as you always did, 'Do I look all right, Dad?'

- Karen's dad

The generation **chasm**

We've had the same old argument again, Dad.
About my clothes. Too much black and much too
long. And you wouldn't take me in the car today
because you can't bear what I look like. Dad, do you
know what that does to me?

You've always taught me to do what's right and to
be my own person. But it seems that you don't want
that to extend to my clothes. That I'm not allowed
to choose what I feel suits me. Or say what I want to
say to the world about who I am. You want me to be
'acceptable' you say. 'Acceptable' to who, Dad? To
your idea of what a well dressed teenage daughter
should look like? I know you mean well and that
you want to be proud of me. But can't you see that
when you criticise the way I dress, you strike at the
very heart of who I am? Of what makes me me?

If I embarrass you, I'm sorry. But just for now,
this is the 'me' I want to be. Please let that 'me'
be acceptable.

- Anna, aged 15

Children today are tyrants. They contradict their parents, gobble their food and tyrannise their teachers.

– Socrates (425-399 BC)

They weren't just **being boring**

I can remember so clearly getting my first job. My friend and I were the envy of the whole school. Somehow we had managed to get a job in a restaurant that joined on to the most well-known nightclub in town. My parents, however, did not share this enthusiasm with me.

"You're not working in a place filled with drunks" was a favourite line of my mother's, or "I'm not having you coming in at all hours of the morning" was a popular moan from my father. I just couldn't understand what the problem was. I had got myself a job – something which they had moaned about me not having – and now I had one, they still moaned. Parents – I just couldn't work them out.

The good thing is that after I had exploded we talked about it. It was two years ago now and at the time I was so sure I was right. Looking back now I have to admit they weren't just being boring. It wasn't a brilliant place for a fifteen-year-old.

- Chloe, aged 17

Lloyd, I've still got a few more questions:

1. Why did the girl of your dreams get an MP3 player for her birthday and I got a packet of chrysanthemum seeds (out of date)?

2. Why do I always get my Father's Day card on the following Tuesday?

3. Why are your A-level notes a mess and your address book immaculate?

4. Why do you save your brightest smiles, wittiest conversation, and offers of help with the washing up for other kids' parents?

5. If the above parents think you're so great, would they consider swapping for a week? I say this in the hope that this would confuse you and you'd suddenly smile at home by mistake.

My kids are always telling me to get a life. But if I had their lives, I'd be dead.

– Calvin Smoot

REPORT CARD

COMPLETED BY:

Lily

AGE:

10 YEARS

SUBJECT	COMMENTS
BEDTIMES	Dad could improve on his school night bedtimes. But Dad is generous on weekend nights. Mum is the same.
FUN	Dad and Mum could both improve on fun on weekdays. On weekends, they're OK but still could improve a bit.
POCKET MONEY	They definitely need to work on pocket money; we don't get any unless we do stuff to help around the house.
FAIRNESS	Mum and Dad are usually fair but sometimes they let my younger brother stay up later than me watching the football. So unfair.
GRUMPINESS	Mum and Dad are both usually grumpy only sometimes are in a good mood. But I guess that's what adults do. They both definitely need to be a bit more smiley sometimes.
COOKING	Mum and Dad are both amazing cooks and cook delicious meals for me. They don't need to work on the cooking skills.

Some thoughts from a **fifteen-year-old**

Kids need a place of their own. Privacy means a lot. Sometimes you just want to be left on your own ... other times you need to talk. It really gets to me when my parents come into my room and start having a go about the state of it.

What is really hard is when your parents disapprove of the boy you're going out with. I think it's a big mistake when parents insist you break up with them because that just makes you want to go out with them even more. In fact, if my mother told me she liked my boyfriend, I'd finish with him on the spot.

You may not agree with your kid's music, but don't mock it – it's a big mistake. You'll lose respect.

I'm proud you're my **daughter**

I want you to know how proud I was of you tonight getting that special prize at school. Your mum would have been too. I had trouble keeping back the tears sitting at the back of the hall – mostly because I didn't want to embarrass you in front of your friends. But I was so proud. Darling, I think they clapped that hard because they knew what you've been through to get this far. They knew the pain you went through when Mum died and the way you've been determined not to let her down. I think maybe somewhere she is feeling just like I am now.

I want you to know that even if you hadn't been up on that stage I would still be bursting with pride! You are growing up into the kind of young woman your mum and I always dreamed you would be. Maybe you haven't done it by the route we'd hoped and it's been a bit stormier than we would have chosen. I'm sure there will always be times like that. But just for now, I want to say I'm proud that you're my daughter.

- Jo's dad, David

REPORT CARD

COMPLETED BY:

Harry

AGE:

11 YEARS

SUBJECT	COMMENTS
BEDTIMES	My parents are generous with what time I go to bed but some of my friends game till 1.00 am, so I still wish I could do that.
FAIRNESS	Although I do sometimes get frustrated with my parents, they are normally very fair with things.
GRUMPINESS	My parents are only grumpy if something upsets them (or someone) and are usually not grumpy and in an OK mood.
COOKING	My mum cooks most and even though Mon-Thu are normal meals, Fri-Sun are treat meals. Mum is a good cook but we have had the occasional disaster.
POCKET MONEY	My parents are generous with pocket money and give £3 every week. They also increase that by £0.50 every year. However saying that every kid would want more pocket money.

Dad, I've got a confession. I always used to think that other kids' parents were much more cool that you and Mum. In fact I used to find you quite embarrassing. And then when I was about sixteen I realised something that seemed impossible: my friends liked you. Some of them said they even liked you more than their own parents. That was a bit strange because I had liked their parents more than you! I suppose it's easier to like somebody when you don't have to live with them. Anyway, I've decided you're not so bad.

Any chance of a new pair of trainers?

Kids tell it like it is on the big issues ...

Brothers and sisters

I wish my mum knew how it feels to me when she spends so much time with my sister. I know she is younger and needs lots of attention, but so do I. Mum spends ages playing dolls with her, but she never plays with me. She says she doesn't know how to play with boys' stuff and that I can do it on my own. But I could show her and it's more fun with two. I know she loves me but I feel as if Lucy is more important because she's a girl.

Marked for life – **Sarah's view**

It took weeks to pluck up courage to get the tattoo done. I'd never do something really big or anything. I just fancied something small and arty and tasteful. So I had a little butterfly done at the top of my arm. I hid it from my mum for weeks and just showed my friends in the cloakroom at school. Then when it got really hot I forgot one day and she saw it under my strap! You'd have thought I'd murdered my granny, the way she went on. It was really no big deal to me any more. I'd done it. I was able to stay calm. Mum went on and on and I just thought it was funny. After all, it's only a little drawing. OK, it won't come off but I know that and it's up to me to live with it. I need to take some responsibility and she needs to lighten up. What's the big deal?

Marked for life – **Sarah's Mum**

I know I might have overreacted. If I did, I'm sorry. I'm sure having a butterfly on your shoulder won't contribute to World War Three. It's just that for a while it seemed like it. You see, you're so precious to me. I know you cringe when I say that, but you are. It's as if I don't want anything to spoil you. And it's not just that it will never come off, without a lot of pain and expense. If that's your style, that's your choice, I can't change that. The hardest thing is that you hid it from me. And that you didn't feel that you could ask my opinion first. I suppose that's because you knew I'd shout. And I did, didn't I? Can we call a truce on this? Can I ask that when you get the snake done on your leg you'll share it with me first?
(Only joking ... please?)

Trapped and **scared**

I was fourteen when I discovered I was pregnant. It was awful. My friend helped me do the test at school and stayed with me all day while I cried and cried. I couldn't believe the ring was blue. I kept thinking that if I looked away, when I looked again it would be gone. My boyfriend was just scared stiff, so I had to think what to do on my own. My friend persuaded me to tell my mum and dad and came with me when I did. She was brilliant. It took me ages to pluck up the courage.

I kept practising how I'd tell them, but in the end I just blurted it out quick and my friend said the rest while I cried. My mum burst into tears and my dad went out of the room. He was really angry with Tim and wanted to go round there. But in the end we all had a good cry together and talked it all out. I felt so much better afterwards and although I knew they were very hurt and angry, in a way it was a good time for us. They helped me think what I'd do and really supported me. I was so glad I'd told them, but it was awful until I did. I just felt trapped and scared.

- Debbie, aged 16

Lloyd, I have a secret wish that is dear to my heart. It's not for more money, or for a sudden reversal of the greying process, or greater success at work. It's more basic than that. Lloyd, I want to see you with teenagers of your own. It doesn't much matter if I'm gasping my last when it happens so long as my hearing is good enough to hear you say, 'No – I want you in at eleven,' or 'No – you can't go out. Do your homework first,' or just 'No.'

I want to be there when your teenager whines, groans, and huffs and puffs. I fully realise that by then I may be very near eternity and my mind should probably be on higher things, but I honestly think if I could be there whilst you have a stand-up row over the state of his bedroom, I could die happy.

Dad, if that would really make you happy I'll give up my A-levels and get married next week. We'll have kids as fast as possible; try to hang on.

There's nothing wrong with teenagers that trying to reason with them won't aggravate.

— Weary mum

It must be a **hard job**

Parents need to understand that we want
to stay out late and we want somebody to
care that we come in on time. We don't want
anybody nagging us over homework and
yet we want somebody to push us a bit to
get it done. We're too old to be hugged but
sometimes we want to be. We can do it all
ourselves and we feel sometimes like kids in
junior school again. We want to be free and
still know you're on guard. Parenting must be
a hard job.

- Kerry, aged 15

More thoughts from a **fifteen-year-old**

It's really dumb when parents say, 'If you have an early night you'll be fresh in the morning' (they make you sound like a lettuce).

And even dumber when they say, 'Do all your homework in the first week of the summer holidays, then you can really enjoy the vacation.' Why break with the tradition of thousands of school kids who've done it on the way to school on the first day of term?

I always remember my father saying, 'It's what people are like inside that counts.' One day we were walking through a subway and there was a homeless man sitting in a sleeping bag playing an old guitar. When my dad didn't give him any money, I asked him why and he said he didn't like the look of him. He always says, 'It's what's inside that counts' then he does that. It's hypocritical.

Sarcastic comments really annoy me – it's the last thing you need when you're in a bad mood.

Little kids' great achievements

I can eat a jam doughnut without licking my lips.

My brother can eat a whole slice of toast in one bite.

The highlight of my childhood was making my brother laugh so hard that food came out of his nose.

I can carry forty-eight conkers in my trouser pockets. Sixty-three if they've got holes in and I've got my green boxer shorts on!

I can spit further than anyone else in my class, even Paul Fielding and he's 4 foot 10.

Being **there**

I can remember when I was seventeen and I went through a really bad bout of depression. My mum tried hard to understand, but she really couldn't. She coped with it by hoovering the carpet eight times in a day and doing lots of cooking.

But my dad was brilliant. He just sat with me. Just sat. Didn't say anything unless I wanted him to, and he held me when I wanted to cry. One sunny day he suggested a drive and we just drove around all the country lanes near where we lived. He never lectured, never got impatient. He helped me unravel the knots inside my head. As I look back now I realise he hardly said anything. He did it by just being there, making me feel I was worth it, and not giving up.

- Jane, aged 18

**Don't limit a child to your own learning,
for he was born in another time.**

– Rabbinic saying

Lloyd, I came across these tips from other fathers – I wish I'd learnt them earlier.

1. Don't take all the credit, don't take all the blame.

2. The life they actually live and the life you perceive them to be living is not the same life.

3. Don't read their school reports as though they are a prophecy of their future lives.

4. Dirt and mess are a breeding ground for well being.

5. Stay out of their rooms after puberty.

6. Never assume that you know your children so well that they can't surprise you anymore.

7. Don't worry that they never listen to you; worry that they are always watching you.

8. Learn from them; they have much to teach you.

9. Love them long; let them go early.

10. Don't keep scorecards on them – a short memory is useful.

Adolescence is a time of rapid ageing. Between the ages of thirteen and nineteen, a parent ages twenty years.

– Tired father

Dad, why do parents give teenagers such a hard time on getting in early? Don't they understand how that makes us feel when all our friends can stay out late? And offering to pick us up from places is even worse.

Lloyd, let me tell you what it's like to be a parent of a teenager who is constantly pushing the boundaries of what time they have to be in at night. First, contrary to popular belief amongst teenagers, most parents do not want to ruin your whole life. We do not want you to come in hours before your friends and so look odd. While I'm at it, neither do we want to pick you up from parties if that makes you look silly.

But all this is really hard. And it's difficult because as parents we are learning as we go. And we've normally had a few scares. Try to imagine being a parent whose child is late coming home. Let me take you into that mother or father's mind. Our child is fourteen and against our better judgment we have said they can come in at eleven because it's a special birthday party. A friend's mother is due to bring everybody home.

Our son should have been home twenty minutes ago and we are starting to panic. We begin to pace the room and then we make a cup of tea. It's now twenty-five past eleven. We wonder who we should call. We vacillate between not wanting to risk waking up friends' parents at this hour and being prepared to wake up the Prime Minister if necessary. Then we tell ourselves that this is silly and we remember what we were like when we were young. That makes us really panic.

And then at about a quarter to twelve we suddenly descend into a spiral of fear from which there is no escape. We imagine policemen knocking the door. We feel sure that the distant sirens of ambulances have something to do with our offspring. And when the boy does come home with a perfectly proper explanation we feel silly, relieved and angry all in one go. And one reason we give you such a hard time over curfews is that we can't go through that every time.

The trick for teens is easy. In the early years, settle for as good as you can get and get home on time every time. Not five minutes late – early if possible. If you're delayed, ring. Build trust that makes it easier for us to be generous.

OK, Dad, I'll be in dead on time – at 5 am.

Son, a little more cheek and you'll be in dead on time at 5 pm.

Trial by **fire**

Dad and I had been through a series of really awful rows. I'd been yelling and screaming. I'd said some really bad things to him. I didn't mean any of it really, but I was always too proud to say so. One day at the end of a bad time I shut myself in my room and hid under the duvet. Dad just came up to the door and stood outside. He let out a huge sigh and then quietly said from outside, 'Paul, I just don't know how we'll get through this or where we're going, but I do know I love you. You're my son, you mean everything to me and I'm not giving up on you.'

I just blubbed and cried for ages after that. I may not have known it, certainly not admitted it, but it was all I needed to hear at the time and it was a turning-point in the crisis. We don't treat each other lightly now. We remember what we went through and the kind of investment of agony that went into the relationship we've got. Trial by fire, if you like.

- Paul, aged 15

**You know you are getting old
when you are going to bed as
your kids are going out.**

– Anon

Lloyd, this is the story I want you never to forget. This is a modern version of it written by a teenager.

There was once a father who had two boys. The younger one came in one day and said, 'Dad, no offence, but you're taking an age to die; I'd like my share of your will now.'

With no arguments the father gave it to him. The son quickly packed a few things and headed for the big city. He found that with his pockets full, friends came easy. Every night was a party with drinking, gambling and women. But on the same day the money ran out, his friends did the same.

He found it hard to get shelter or a job but finally ended up looking after a herd of pigs. He was so hungry he'd have eaten their food except that the pigs' owner was more concerned about keeping the pigs alive than him. One night he woke up to reality and said, 'I'm going home. Even my father's servants have a meal to eat and a roof over their heads. I'll tell him I've blown it as his son, but beg him for a job around the farm.'

And so he began his long walk home. What he didn't know was that every day the old man had looked down the road waiting for his boy to come back. And when he saw his son in the distance he began to run. The boy tried to make his speech but his father didn't let him finish – instead he was yelling, 'Put a robe on his back, and some shoes on his feet, and get a ring on his finger. And while you're at it, get a party ready. The boy's come home!'

Meanwhile the older brother was working nearby. He heard the rumpus and asked a worker, 'What's going on?' He got the news that his brother had come back and the old man had thrown a party. He went right into a major sulk and point blank refused to come to the celebrations. The father came out to persuade him to come in, but got an earful instead: 'I've never given you a hard time – been the perfect child – and you've never given me a party. Now the waster has come back and you go to town on him.'

The old man said, 'Son, you are both equal to me but you have both made mistakes and your brother has realised his and returned. Please forgive him as I have done and join the party – he was dead but now he's alive again. He was lost and now he's found. Your brother's home.'

Lloyd, be honest with me, are you glad or not that I pushed you so much to get those GCSEs? It was like shoving blancmange up a hill. I remember that one day when I literally locked you in a neighbour's house to learn 'Emmeline Pankhurst and the Suffragettes.'

Dad, as much as I hate to admit it: Yes.

The undoubted champion stupidest thing ever said by any **parent** ever

What did you do in school today?

Some more lessons every **parent** needs to know

The spin cycle on a washing machine does not make earthworms dizzy ...

... it will however make cats dizzy.

Cats throw up twice their body weight when dizzy.

Lloyd, when you were small we used to play a game. I would be on my deathbed and trying to tell you with my few last breaths where I had hidden all my treasure. You would lean in close as I mumbled, 'It's in the ...'

You would shout, 'It's in the what?'

I would stutter, 'It's in the blue ...'

'It's in the blue what? Chest? Coat? Ocean? What?'

'It's in the blue box that is under the ...'

I would normally play you along for ten minutes or so, get you tantalisingly close and then finally close my eyes forever. I have often wondered whether you were just playing along or it really was only the money you cared about.

But now I want to play the game again – except this time you'll get all the answers. When I'm gone these are ten things I want you to remember forever.

1. It's not true that anybody can achieve anything, but most of us can achieve beyond our wildest dreams.

2. Treat people with dignity, especially those who work in jobs that others consider menial.

3. Never forget the parable of the prodigal son that Jesus told. No matter what you have done, you can always come home.

4. Remember that many people have suffered because a bank manager has said 'No', but thousands more because a bank manager said, 'Yes.'

5. Stay in touch with your sister Kate. It's sad when families lose touch – be there for each other.

6. If you have kids of your own, let them know you love them irrespective of their achievements. Don't be so busy working to give them what you didn't have that you don't have time to give them what you did have.

7. Try not to be always asking, "What do other people think of me?" It will imprison you.

8. If you marry, be faithful.

9. Try to forgive. The Chinese proverb is right: 'The man who will not forgive must dig two graves.'

10. Always believe that this life is not all there is. It will give you a sense of perspective both in good times and bad. More important, it will give you hope.

Lloyd, this has been a fun book to do together and we've both tried not to get too serious. But I want to tell you that you are not just a son to me; you have become a friend. I have so many hopes for you – that you reach your potential whatever that may be, that you make a difference in the lives of those who are weak, that you keep the faith. But I also want you to know that my love for you is not based on whether you please me or not. I confess that pleasing me will make that love a little easier, but in truth I will love you anyway. That is irrational, perhaps even foolish, and exactly the way most parents feel.

And as we come to the end of our great effort, I have only one desire: it is that just as over the past years you have quoted back at me every word I have ever uttered on parenting, so I pray that one day your child will find this book. And, Lloyd, if I am gone when that moment occurs, listen hard, because you'll hear me laughing on the wind.

Dad, that is one of the most moving things I have ever heard.
Could you lend me a tenner?

... and vice versa

Rob Parsons, OBE, is the Chairman and Founder of Care for the Family. He has spoken across the world on family issues and is the author of many books including the *Sixty Minute* series.

Rob is married to Dianne, lives in Cardiff in South Wales and has two adult children and five grandchildren.

About Care for the Family

Established in 1988, Care for the Family is a charity based in the UK, but with an increasing reach internationally. We support parents, couples and those who are bereaved, through events, courses, podcasts, volunteer befrienders, books and other evidence-based, accessible resources.

cff.org.uk